Dashel

the

Darling Dachshund

By Dawn Roe

A Pap's Pups Book

By Dawn Roe

Dashel the Darling Dachshund by Dawn Roe

Copyright © 2019. All rights reserved.

ALL RIGHTS RESERVED: No part of this book may be reproduced, stored, or transmitted, in any form, without the express and prior permission in writing of Pen It! Publications. This book may not be circulated in any form of binding or cover other than that in which it is currently published.

This book is licensed for your personal enjoyment only. All rights are reserved. Pen It! Publications does not grant you rights to resell or distribute this book without prior written consent of both Pen It! Publications and the copyright owner of this book. This book must not be copied, transferred, sold or distributed in any way.

Disclaimer: Neither Pen It! Publications, or our authors will be responsible for repercussions to anyone who utilizes the subject of this book for illegal, immoral or unethical use.

This is a work of fiction. The views expressed herein do not necessarily reflect that of the publisher.

This book or part thereof may not be reproduced in any form, stored in a retrieval system, or transmitted in any form by any means-electronic, mechanical, photocopy, recording or otherwise-without prior written consent of the publisher, except as provided by United States of America copyright law.

Published by Pen It! Publications, LLC
812-371-4128   www.penitpublications.com

Published in the United States of America by Pen It! Publications, LLC

ISBN: 978-1-951263-73-7

Pictures provided by Author

He was born in our kitchen, two sisters, one brother. Our black and tan doxie was Sydney, his mother.

The first pup to play and jump off of the chair, Dash would let out a bark and then fly through the air!

When his brother and sisters had all found new homes, he stayed with his Mommy and nursed all alone.

Then as he got bigger and we had our first snow, he'd jump on a sled and down the hill he would go!

Then he'd ride the snowboard and sled on the ice. In a basket up front, he'd even ride on our bikes.

When he'd hear our piano, Dash jumped up on the seat. He'd stand on the keys
And play it with me.

For a really fun trick, we'd pick up that dog and let him ride on the back of our big dirty hog.

When I would yell "squacky!" he'd run to a tree to look for a squirrel,

And then he'd run back to me.

He found there were rats out there on the farm, so he'd dig, dig, dig, dig his way round the barn. With a bark and a wag, he'd show Pap the way to find where they were.

He would do it all day.

He was never afraid until he heard a gun, and then off he would go. Back home he would run!

But when it was time to all go to bed,
he'd lick clean his coat and snuggle next to my head.

Protecting his home and his family too, are some of his favorite things he can do.

He's loyal and true and beautiful too. I think Dashel's the most darling dog.

Don't you?

The End

**Author Dawn Roe** is a wife, mother and Mimi in southern Ohio. She works part of the year as an Assistant Teacher to Preschoolers. The rest of the year she spends with family. She loves traveling, kayaking, fishing and photographing life, as it happens.

Writing songs and poetry has always been a part of her life and she is now ready to share it with others.

Milton Keynes UK
Ingram Content Group UK Ltd.
UKHW022054240324
440008UK00002B/39